Shakeela Hassan
2/29/2020

A Starry Crown

Making

of a *Fez*

A Symbol of Distinction and Evolution

for

Leadership of Hon. Elijah Muhammad

The Leader of the Nation of Islam

Shakeela Z. Hassan, MD

Harran Productions Foundation - Chicago

A Starry Crown- Making of a *Fez*

A Symbol of Distinction and Evolution
for Leadership of Hon. Elijah Muhammad
The Leader of the Nation of Islam

Published by Harran Productions Foundation

Chicago, IL 60611

www.harranfoundation.org

ISBN: 978-1-6774-2408-5

Library of Congress Control Number: 2019913439

Book Cover Design: Kwame Thomas: Kwamination.com

Cover photo of the Fez: Guclu Koseli: Chicago Visual

Transcription of initial recordings: Ahmed Ali

Printed in the United States of America

DEDICATION

A Special Acknowledgement
Late M. Zia Hassan

With much love and a heavy heart, it is important for me to share the life of my dear husband, the *Late* Professor M. Zia Hassan. Zia played an intricate part in designing the Fez. From a random plan to its perfection of details, the Fez became a permanent iconic presence for the distinguished Leader of the Nation of Islam, The Honorable Elijah Muhammad. I acknowledge him as a co-author, architect and a catalyst for all the amazing goodness we witnessed together. It was an honor and privilege to be his wife. *Thank God, Alhamdulillah!*

How did Shakeela and Zia meet? We met in Chicago. We are Muslims but come from two different Muslim families, Zia a Punjabi from Lahore, Pakistan and Shakeela, a Hyderabadi from Hyderabad, British India.

In essence, our life together is a story of how two young people met, fell in love, and became an integral part of history in defining the legacy of The Honorable Elijah Muhammad.

As *Late* Zia Hassan reflected on his life, and its meaning and interpretation, he knew that the smooth journey and chance encounters were a part of "God's Plan".

We were destined to be together. Sixty beautiful years of marriage, a partnership of a lifetime, and a love that stood the test of time. When asked many years later by one of our granddaughters (Ayla Mian) how "Nana (grandfather) met Nani (grandmother)" Zia simply said, "When I saw her, I said, she is my wife."

This was no surprise to me. It was a confirmation of how naturally our lives were forming. For the next 60 years, we were gratefully blessed to be together as a team. What an extraordinary encounter of two seemingly ordinary people 'striving to be peaceful humans' in this journey called life.

Alhamdulillah, Thanks Be to God.

Zia transitioned on October 29, 2017.

I end with a deep sense of loss of my husband. His love, support and care for me is undeniable. Zia's profound life message was an inspiration for many people.

"Life is a journey of perpetual quality improvement." ~Zia Hassan

When asked what his thoughts were on meeting and getting to know the Elijah Muhammad family and their community, Zia responded "To have a relationship with trust, honesty, and respect has been a blessing for me and my wife." I believe it is "God's Plan."

Zia was God's gift to me. I am profoundly grateful to *Allah Subhana wa ta'ala (Glory Be to God)*, and to our family, community and all who share in God's purposefully created diverse human family.

"Verily, we are Almighty God's and verily to Him shall we return." (Qur'an 2:156)

Shakeela Z. Hassan, MD

TABLE OF CONTENTS

Shakeela Z. Hassan, MD

FOREWORD

With Allah's Name, The Merciful Benefactor, The Merciful Redeemer

The history and existence of the original Nation of Islam and its leader has been obscured from the pages of history in America along with the Honorable Elijah Muhammad, the leader of the Nation of Islam. My grandfather was known for his fiery messages of Black Nationalism. He was the greatest social reformer in history. His message, to his people, required them to become Muslims and abandon false practices. He was an evolved leader who only had a third-grade education. His teacher, Professor Fard, aka Master Fard, introduced him to a strange and peculiar form of Islam. Elijah Muhammad would come to understand that his people needed more than a wake-up message to save them from mental slavery. He began to search for new ways to guide his congregation of followers to a better state of mind and purpose. In his quest for progress, his prayers were answered. His life would take a new and fresh turn of events, aided by a young couple from India.

It was in the mid 1950's that Zia and Shakeela Hassan would enter the lives of Elijah and Clara Muhammad. Zia Hassan met my grandfather. He gazed upon an astonishing man and was captivated by his humble demeanor and his kindness. Zia Hassan would soon invite his future wife to answer an invitation to meet Elijah and Clara Muhammad in their Chicago home. This was the beginning of a lifetime relationship between the two couples. Only The Will of G-d could have brought about what would unfold into a marvelous epiphany.

A Starry Crown

A Starry Crown (the making of the Fez) takes the reader on a journey through the life and times of the Honorable Elijah Muhammad and one of the most unique and loving relationships known in modern day history. You, perhaps, will never find anything so amazing and delightfully written about true friendship and everlasting love.

Halimah Muhammad-Ali

Shakeela Z. Hassan, MD

Preface

The Fez is complicated in origin, beautiful on the head, unpopular in modern times, but has seen more glorious days. From the time it was worn by the Moroccans during protests against French invasion to the period when men in Libya and Egypt were jailed for wearing them, the Fez has moved with revolutions and has become popular or unpopular, in relation to those in power.

The origin of the Fez hat can be traced to the spread of the Ottoman Empire; it is however argued that it has its real origin in Morocco. Fez is the name of the main town of Morocco. The Fez is also known as 'tarboosh' or 'checheya' and it is mostly made of felt or rough woven fabrics. Fez hats are brimless and are either shaped like a short cylinder or a truncated cone, attached with a tassel on top and worn either alone or with a turban.

Fez hats have history as deep as most Eastern parts of the world. The Fez has seen the invasion of certain eastern states. When a regime seizes the government, they always ban or resurrect the popularity of the Fez. Therefore, this elusive hat can be said to be political, social, and historic.

Well, history has its place. Journey with me as I take you back 60 years to a special moment where me and my husband Zia created our own brand of history.

"In the Name of God, Amazingly Merciful, Infinitely Compassionate," to
"Thanks Be to God" - every step of the way.

Introduction

Is there any way to predict how a dining table conversation would materialize into designing a Fez, "A Starry Crown"? The head gear referred to as his Fez, became a historic iconic symbol and personal defining mark of distinction for The Honorable Elijah Muhammad, the leader of The Nation of Islam.

Hon. Elijah Muhammad addressing Nation of Islam Convention

At the International Amphitheater in Chicago, February 1961

Alif Muhammad, Sr., grandson of the Hon. Elijah Muhammad and President of HEMCC Foundation

Not only was this a mark of distinction, it personified his message. In hindsight, Brother Muhammad wanted to refresh his image and that's exactly what happened. After all, every iconic image has its beginning. In 1961, he contemplated adding a special touch to his appearance. As the story unfolds, we learned the value of communication, forthright interactions and volunteer participation. These traits were instrumental as a precursor for teamwork and the realization of a dream. A vision, an answer to questions, producing results, all because of a man who desired change. What amazing grace!

I gratefully refer to it as "God's Will," the fruition of a purposeful encounter and the result of working together to formulate and produce results. The noteworthy simplicity, unpredicted chance encounters, and human interactions complement and set the stage for a Fez in the making. Perhaps, it is fair to say, "Yes, it was meant to be!"

Writing about the beginning stages of development of the Fez, drew my attention to how swift and serene this journey has been for me. With all due respect and rationale, the term "Fez" will be used in sharing my story. Brother Elijah flashed his signature smile every time he called it a Fez, and each time he wore it he did what he loved to do, leading his community to faith and righteousness for common good, faith and responsibility.

The Making of the Fez

The Fez, as Brother Muhammad wished to call it, is a story about a hat that was created as a result of a chance encounter that took place between my husband, Dr. Zia Hassan and myself at the dinner table of Brother Elijah Muhammad and Sister Clara Muhammad.

A Starry Crown

He wore the Fez on regular and special occasions while meeting and greeting dignitaries, local, national and international leaders and visitors. It was specially a part of his presence on stage while addressing his audience. The annual Saviour's Day Convention, in February 1961, attracted a significantly larger number of Nation of Islam followers in attendance, eager to meet the Leader and pay him respect.

There he was, wearing the specially designed Fez, an embroidered embellished velvet cap. Remarkably, it was not commissioned, requested or even discussed in any prior conversation or interaction. Until, of course, I came along.

The cap – the Fez, reached its historic and iconic presence over the past almost six decades, as a hallmark of the leadership brand of the Nation of Islam's leader, The Honorable Elijah Muhammad. In my recollection, to the best of my knowledge, a spontaneous, unexpected turn of events defined a chance encounter and an inadvertent conversation from the heart turned an ordinary moment into an extraordinary historic milestone. This is etched in my memory. It gives me a sense of humbling pride and blessed joy to say, Zia and I became part and parcel of the evolving strength, and Mark of Distinction of the Leadership of Honorable Elijah Muhammad for six decades.

All Praise Be to God, Subhan Allah!!

I did not dwell on how and why these events occurred. I am convinced, whatever happens, happens for a reason. It's God's Will after all. In life, we must capture each moment, listen attentively and do the best we can with what we have.

Shakeela Z. Hassan, MD

The Fez

A Starry Crown 1960

Photo Credit: Guclu Koseli, Chicago Visual

CHAPTER 1

A Chance Encounter

I will set the stage of a remarkable story that began as follows. Upon arriving in Chicago from Pakistan in 1955, Zia attended the Illinois Institute of Technology for a postgraduate education. In June 1956, I arrived in Chicago for my postgraduate medical training at Northwestern University's Evanston Hospital in Evanston, Illinois.

In early August 1956, two strangers, Zia from Lahore, Pakistan, and me from Hyderabad, British India, met by chance (or by destiny as some would call it) at a professor's home. A faculty member from Illinois Institute of Technology and his wife hosted a group of 'foreign students' from the greater Chicago area in their home for dinner.

On August 14, 1956, Zia invited me to attend Pakistan Independence Day Celebration, which was held at the University of Chicago's International House. After joining Zia, he casually mentioned that he met Brother Elijah Muhammad, and his wife, Sister Clara Muhammad. He said, "They are very nice people. They are Black Muslims in the Nation of Islam. I spoke to them about you and they are keen to meet you." He added, "I am sure you would like them." His statements did not baffle or concern me, nor did I question him. I was unfamiliar with Black Muslims and the Nation of Islam. In hindsight, my thoughts were twofold. Firstly, I was so enchanted and comfortable with Zia, that I respected and trusted him completely. Secondly, the chain of events and chance encounters with Zia were convincingly clear that I should get used to the idea

"It is going be to be what it is going to be – God's Plan." I had no concerns or questions about their color or their ethnicity and felt comfortable and looked forward to our meeting. The question never entered my mind. In reflection, Zia's comfort with the situation paved the path for a mutually joyous experience of a life-long friendship.

Hon. Elijah & Sister Clara Muhammad's Residence, 4847 Woodlawn Ave.

Photo Credit: Alif Muhammad, Sr., grandson of the Hon. Elijah Muhammad and President of HEMCC Foundation

Barely knowing one another, I accepted Zia's invitation to meet the Muhamad's – no questions asked. It was the end of August 1956. I was very young, confident and comfortable to be with Zia. He arrived several days later, in the evening, and pulled up to the hospital campus where I resided in the house-staff quarters. Helen Dulick, a woman director for our house staff program, approached me and announced, "Hey Shakeela, a dashing young man has arrived to see you, and guess what – he is driving a yellow Cadillac."

In the car, he told me a bit more and we arrived at 4847 Woodlawn Avenue, in Chicago's Kenwood neighborhood. Zia parked the car as two guards guided him. Afterwards, they respectfully ushered us to the front entrance. The door opened and Brother Elijah and Sister Clara were standing at the door with big smiles and looked very happy to welcome us into their home. They greeted us with a customary Muslim greeting, "*Assalamualaikum*" *(peace be unto you)* and we responded with "*Waalaikumassalam*" *(and upon you be peace).*

This was necessary as it set the stage for mutual comfort and peace. Sister Clara gave me a warm hug and pecks on my cheeks. She held my hand and guided me through the foyer into the living room. It was so charming, calming and comforting to meet a family who welcomed us graciously and extended their hospitality. No one asked me questions about my name, my ancestry, or if I was familiar with one thing or the other. Brother Elijah and Sister Clara quickly won my respect as elders. In retrospect, it simply was an attestation of their fondness and comfort with Zia.

Meeting Halimah

Granddaughter of Elijah and Clara Muhammad

As usual Halimah and I were having a great time reminiscing and travelling down memory lane. Realizing when she and I literally first 'met' or laid eyes on one another is historically significant. Halimah, **out of the blue asked** "Share with me, what you remember when you came to my grandparents' home with Dr. Zia – your husband, the very first time. Tell me all the details."

I said, "Halimah, let me first clarify that Zia and I were not married, we barely knew one other, I had just come to the states to start my post graduate training in June 1956 in Medicine at the Northwestern University in Evanston. I came to 4847 Woodlawn Avenue, to your grandparents' home in end of August, 1956. When we came to the door, your lovely grandparents graciously welcomed us with open arms and happy hearts." Halimah was excitedly impatient for me to fast forward and share what else I saw or heard. With equal excitement, I said, "There were more people in the house, some children too. I did see a little girl standing closely against the wall in front of me."

Halimah exclaimed, "That was me, I was six years old!" adding, "I couldn't help it – I was so excited to see you both to the house and saw how my grandparents brought you in so happily." In the mean time I was super excited and thinking, "Who are these people? I have seen some Caucasians and black people but no one looking so beautiful and unique than these two." Then she said to me, "You had beautiful long hair- apparently referring to my full head of hair in a good-sized bun." She remarked about my colorful clothes and about Zia, so well dressed and good looking. The thing to be shared is another human check and balance. She then said, "I was in such awe, I was in a stunned state with my eyes wide open and my body position in a state of surprise". She said, my cousin who was a young teenager at that time, came from behind and tapped me on my shoulder saying "Cousin, STOP, stop, You are staring, it is Bad Manners!"

We both felt a shudder down our spines, memories frozen vividly in time and emotion. I quickly added, "Was that Sharon, your aunt Ethel's daughter?" She said, "YES." I fondly recall how Sister Ethel Eaa and Sister Lottie Rayya's daughters visited their grandparents most frequently. Again, it is noteworthy that their moms, Sister Ethel Eaa and Sister Lottie Rayya were regular participants in conversations and carrying out of projects for the Nation of Islam Community and families.

Over a period of time, Brother Elijah Muhammad and Sister Clara became the elders, or parental figures, in our lives. For me, Sister Clara was personally supportive and helped me in times of my homesickness and missing of my own mother. She always made me feel comfortable and special.

Halimah As a Child at About Age Six

Shakeela and Zia in 1957

The pictures above:

1. Halimah, age 6 approximately, was the big eyes of wonder with a broad smile. She was on a journey to become the family historian and recalls how her beloved Grandmother was her hero. Halimah and I met totally by chance and fell in "like at first sight".

2. This is a photo of Zia and me taken in 1957. I was approximately 20 years old. We both were in our own wonderlands but seem happy to go along with whatever came before us on individual fronts of life and its deliberations. Little did we know what lay ahead decades later as we have been in touch one way or the other – early on at THE HOUSE and later as opportunities permitted.

In the last decade, Halimah's love and commitment to be her family's historian inspired us to interact and converse frequently.

Women who actively participate in various roles and capacities of leadership, including the recording and preservation of history, have roles that need to be enhanced and energized in a prevalent Man's world.

Historically, it is a journey of such moments and encounters that continued to enrich my life while involved in learning, loving and living the lessons learnt and to make progress in faith and servitude. Through the process of growth and passage of time, it is precious to realize how God's Will paves the path and leads the way by giving us a roadmap in our life's journey. *"Where there is a Will. There is a Way."*

Prior to Zia's transition, he shared that there were several interest groups and individuals who wanted to hear our story. Zia's response was "When I arrived in

Chicago, I did not know the Muhammads. I met them here, I also met my wife here. I introduced her to them, they loved us both, my wife loved them and we both reciprocated their love. Brother knew that my interest was in education. He was fascinated by education and would often run his ideas by me. He trusted me and was at ease with my respect for him. He knew I was doing my best. My wife and I were always available to serve them in matters of education and whatever they felt a need to talk about, at any time or day. We were married in December 1959. In 1960 shortly after our marriage, we were asked to come over for a visit. These visits were for conversations and reflections on a variety of issues. On this particular occasion Brother Elijah Muhammad, Sister Clara, Zia and I proceeded to the dining room and took our seats and began to converse. Sister Clara and I were catching up with exchange of family news and welfare and Zia was engaged in conversation with Brother Elijah Muhammad. As we conversed, our meeting escalated into a momentous occasion, 'Making of the Fez'.

As I write the story of how the Fez originated, it behooves me to say, without Zia's amazing input about the desired structure to size, fit, comfort, colors, etc., the making of the Fez would not be possible.

Each of the four of us were so comfortable moving forward in hopes that the "Making of the Fez" would produce tangible results. As we progressed, there were no debates, differences of opinion or convincing one another involved. We both believed that our commitments were to be honest, true, and do our best at all times, while respecting their privacy, vision and mission.

Our visits with Brother Elijah and Sister Clara Muhammad's family continued regularly and frequently as time permitted. We were very comfortable socializing with

Brother Elijah and Sister Clara because we connected with them on many levels, *e.g.*, faith, family, friendship, grassroots, service, quest for self-respect, self-reliance, social and moral justice, human rights and civility, respect for others, and finding your sense of responsibility. Education was the key element of consideration in all aspects of vision, commitment and deliberations. This vision was for men, women and children with a focus to build strengths of faith, character, knowledge, fostering responsibility and service as individuals, as families, and together as a community. Brother Elijah and Sister Clara never referred to us with any of the hyphenated distinctions, i.e., immigrants, foreigners – people from other planets or whatever the lingo was during that era or even how it has shaped ever since. Experiential learning, I feel strongly has been a key element. What we learn from one another surpasses any and all you might know or learn from any and all other means.

"O' mankind, Surely We have created you from a male and a female, and made you tribes and families that you may know each other. Surely the noblest of you with Allah is the most dutiful of you. Surely Allah is Knowing, Aware."

~Holy Qur'an Surah Al-Hujurat 49:13

Shakeela Z. Hassan, MD

Shakeela and Zia Hassan in their home at 4847 Woodlawn Avenue, Chicago

Photographed in 1963

Hon. Elijah Muhammad's Key Message
To
The "Black Man" & the Nation of Islam Community

"The Duty of the Black Man
is
To do for Self and think for Self."
~Hon. Elijah Muhammad

In reflection of our journey of what my husband and I were blessed to travel with, in time, I came to understand the Hon. Elijah and Sister Clara Muhammad's purpose for quality improvement of a community. A community that was dealing with abuse, discrimination and lack of self-respect and so much more.

Hon. Elijah and Sister Clara Muhammad's pursuit and purpose for the historic attempts at social and spiritual reform of the Black community was the energy and sense, that personally furthered, enlightened, inspired and kept our admiration captured, to focus on the good!

"O' you who believe, let not people laugh at people, perchance they may be better than they; nor let women (laugh) at women, perchance they may be better than they. Neither find fault with your own people, nor call one another by nicknames. Evil is a bad name after faith; and whoso turns not, these it is that are the iniquitous."

~Holy Qur'an, Surah 49 Verse 11

CHAPTER 2

Brother Elijah Muhammad Visits Lahore

In late December 1959, The Honorable Elijah Muhammad along with his sons, Herbert (Jabir Muhammad), Elijah Muhammad II, Akbar Muhammad, and several others, travelled to Mecca Saudi Arabia, for Umrah (Mini Pilgrimage) and visited Lahore Pakistan. The group also visited Africa. While in Lahore Pakistan, they visited Mian Izhar-ul Hassan and his wife, Walayat Begum (Parents of the Hassan brothers). They resided in Krishan Nagar on Hearne Road. Zia's parents hosted a dinner in their honor. Several members of the family were there to meet, greet and honor The Honorable Elijah Muhammad and his sons. Zia's parents presented a Jinnah Cap to The Honorable Elijah Muhammad. A Jinnah cap is a special Qaraquli hat, named after the Founder of Pakistan, Mr. Muhammad Ali Jinnah who wore it for the first time in 1937.

Shakeela Z. Hassan, MD

Wearing the Jinnah Cap

Honorable Elijah Muhammad

Mohammad Ali Jinnah

M. Zia Hassan

Dr. Ijaz-ul-Hassan (Zia's older brother) introduced Zia to The Honorable Elijah Muhammad. Dr. Hassan, as he was referred to by the Muhammad family) He was in postgraduate Surgical Residency Program at the University of Chicago. He met The Honorable Elijah Muhammad during his clinic visits for some minor issues. They would later meet at the Muhammad's home during his stay in Chicago.

In 1955 during his visit, Dr. Ijaz ul Hassan told brother Elijah that he was about to leave on a short vacation to attend his older brother's wedding back home in Lahore, Pakistan. He also shared that he would be accompanied by his younger brother Zia, who plans to pursue postgraduate education at a University in Chicago. Brother Muhammad asked about his travel itinerary details and said, "I will make arrangements for both of you to be taken care of in New York; someone will pick you up at the airport when you land and take you to the other airport for the connecting flight to Chicago." This was a very thoughtful and helpful gesture, as there were no direct flights to Chicago at that time. Later, I learnt that Malcolm X was the person who met them at the airport and escorted the two Hassan brothers to his home. He showered them with generous acts of hospitality and engaging conversations. When it was time for the next flight, he drove them to the airport, several hours later. His hospitality and mutually memorable time together, are memorable moments of history for our family.

L to R: Akbar Muhammad, Sister Clara Muhammad, Brother Elijah Muhammad, Abdul Basit Naeem, Jabir Herbert Muhammad and Elijah Muhammad Jr.

Photo Credits: Alif Muhammad, Sr. grandson of the Hon. Elijah Muhammad and President of HEMCC Foundation

Zia's youngest brother, Iftikhar Hassan, a teenager at the time, remembered the visit of The Honorable Elijah Muhammad and his team. They visited Zia's family four times and shared dinner together. During their visit, they were also introduced to Sheikh Muhammad Ashraf, the founder and owner of Sheikh Muhammad Ashraf & Son in Lahore, a century old famous publishing company established in 1921. The publishing institution takes pride in being recognized for the English translation of the Holy Qur'an, commentary and notes by Allama Abdullah Yusuf Ali. This was the most popular, and perhaps the first, English translation available at that time. Iftikhar Hassan vividly recalls their visit and also the "Making of the Fez" details in Lahore. He recalls not only receiving the Velvet Fabric along with requested designs and instructions and how he was part of the process to take it to the "Raza Cap" to get them made. He fondly shared receiving many velvet fabric parcels from us in Chicago, over time to get the embroidery done. Muhammad Family visit has been a significant part of fond memories over time for all in the Hassan family.

Dr. Ijaz and Zia had previously presented copies of the Yusuf Ali Translation to The Honorable Elijah Muhammad while visiting Chicago. The meeting with the *Late* Sheikh Mohammad Ashraf, at Zia Hassan's family residence in Lahore, set the stage for acquiring future copies of Yusuf Ali's translation of the Qur'an for The Honorable Elijah Muhammad's group.

In addition to copies of Yusuf Ali's English translation of the Qur'an, other books were written/translated into English which included: hadith, religion and culture, biography and memoirs (Khalifas, Prophets), Islamic books for children and Islamic law. Philosophy and education were also introduced to the Clara Muhammad Schools, formerly, "The University of Islam". The Nation of Islam's education became widespread and adapted in the broader school curricula. The children's books especially, were well received. Halimah Mohammed-Ali, granddaughter of Elijah and Clara Muhammad, remembers the books in her classroom. Halimah says that she and her siblings, cousins and fellow students, recall fondly how they benefitted by learning about Islamic history, including the Prophet Muhammad, Khalifas, and more. She felt comfortable being a Muslim. She recalls how Sister Clara Muhammad (her grandmother) and Sister Lottie Rayya Muhammad, her mother, the daughter of Elijah and Clara Muhammad, were part of the curriculum planning and teachings at the school. Sister Lottie Rayya served as the Director and Dean of the Clara Muhammad School System.

Brother Elijah and Sister Clara held fond regards for me and Zia and became an intricate part of the educational process. Their heartfelt interest in Islamic education served as a precursor to an inadvertent humbling opportunity for Zia and me. It was amazing grace and readiness that Sister Clara and her daughter Sister Lottie Rayya Muhammad were able to integrate the books into the classrooms. and the curriculum. Zia and I felt humbled and happy to be there as we shared all we could and as needed. Team work was always the style of Brother Elijah and Sister Clara Muhammad and their daughters.

After Sh. Ashraf's death in 1981, the Press was passed on to his grandson, Shahzad Riaz (grandson of Mr. Ashraf and son of Mr. Ashraf's daughter - Mrs. Rasheeda Riaz and her husband – Dr. Riaz ul-Hassan, (the oldest of the Hassan brothers). Zia and his older brother, Dr. Ijaz Hassan, are the two that knew Brother Elijah Muhammad.

Dr. Abdus Salam, a dentist for The Honorable Elijah Muhammad, was the one in charge of acquiring and importing copies of Yusuf Ali's English translation of the Qur'an, and other Islamic books, as well as some that were used as children's books.

Dr. Ijaz and Zia had already presented copies of the Yusuf Ali Translation to The Honorable Elijah Muhammad during their visits with him in Chicago. This meeting set the stage for future acquisitions of Yusuf Ali's translation of the Qur'an for the Honorable Elijah Muhammad followers. These transactions continued directly between the parties.

Shakeela Z. Hassan, MD

L-R: Zia Hassan, Hon. Elijah Muhammad & Dr. Ijaz-ul-Hassan

at the Honorable Elijah & Sister Clara's Muhammad's Home in Chicago (1955)

Inscribed copy of Yusuf Ali's English translation of the Qur'an, presented in 1955 to

Hon. Elijah Muhammad by Dr. M. I. Hassan

Photo Credits: Alif Muhammad, Sr., grandson of the Hon. Elijah Muhammad and President of HEMCC Foundation

CHAPTER 3

The Fez

Passage of Time is a Witness: Six Decades Later

A totally random idea out of the blue is visualized and realized with ease, and effort in accomplishing our mission. From a discussion at a table to a trip to Marshall Fields, which highlights the value of the Fez. Before I knew it, the details, the materials with the design sketch and every measurement were sent to Lahore. In a short period, the Fez was created and ready to be worn by Brother Elijah for his upcoming Savior day in 1961. This was his first massive audience.

As I remember how the Fez came into existence, the entire story seems surreal. Just imagine, one fine day, after working night duty at the hospital, coming home to hear my husband say, "Shakeela, we will be visiting Brother and Sister this afternoon. Are you okay with that?" God bless him! He always checked to see if I was available to accompany him to different places.

The Invitation

One Sunday morning Zia and I were invited to Brother Elijah's home for one of our usual gatherings which took place in 1960, shortly after our marriage in December 1959. We arrived at their residence sometime late that Sunday morning and the four of us proceeded to the dining table, which was our usual place to converse or dine with family or guests. Our accustomed seating arrangements had Brother Elijah sitting at the head of the table, Sister Clara to his right, I sat to Sister Clara's right, and Zia sat at Brother Elijah's left, across from Sister Clara. These were our usual seating arrangements unless we were advised differently. In any case, I always sat next to Sister Clara, while Zia at times sat directly across from Brother at the opposite end of the table.

But on this particular occasion, Brother Elijah spoke to my husband Zia about his wardrobe. Sister Clara and I on the other hand happily caught up on our conversations about the welfare of our families, projects and other topics that came to mind. Brother Elijah was busy speaking with Zia. Suddenly, I overheard the intense conversation of the gentlemen regarding Brother Elijah's wardrobe specifics, *e.g.*, the color choices of his suit, appropriate seasonal colors, fabric variations and a need for a different Fez. Brother Elijah always complemented Zia on his apparel. Zia's style was simplicity and clean lines. Brother stated, "I should wear colors other than black." Zia said he prefers browns, blues and grays because they are winter and fall colors.

The conversation piqued my interest when I heard the word Fez. As Brother Elijah placed a cap on the table, he hinted how it would be nice to have a different Fez. This particular one was reddish in color, soft, round and a bit unstructured and floppy. My attention was drawn by Brother Elijah referring to the cap as a Fez.

I felt compelled to interrupt and express my viewpoint. I softly said to sister, almost in a whisper, "Sister, please excuse me," and I raised my hand as I addressed Brother Elijah, as I had learned to do in Montessori kindergarten school. I said, "Pardon me Brother." Brother Elijah responded, "Yes Sister." I said, "Brother, the cap you are referring to as a Fez is not a Fez. A Fez is a classical head covering, headdress, cap or a hat made of red wool felt material, tapered with a long black tassel on one side and truncated cylindrical in shape." Brother was very pleased to engage in a conversation where all four of us were participating. I further explained that it is worn in the city of Fez in Morocco, later in Turkey and in Hyderabad by the Nizams. My family and I grew up in Hyderabad. My father wore a Fez on Nizam's ceremonious occasions and my brothers wore them too. Hyderabad was a princely state in British India before its partition and independence in being India and Pakistan in 1947. Hyderabad lost its Princely status of being under the Asaf Jah Dynasty - being under the rule of Mir Osman Ali Khan, the last Nizam of Hyderabad, Nizam ul-Mulk, also known as Asaf Jah.

History of the Fez

Fez hats have a long and complicated history in the Middle East, Eastern Europe and North Africa. Romans shared the Fez tradition and it is also mentioned to have its presence in Morocco and several Muslim countries. Shriners wore them too.

Nizam also wore this in his holding of the court, receiving celebrity guests and other occasions. For formal occasions and celebrations. The different elaborate and elegant head dress Dastaar was the choice. It was specially made of fine silk fabric layered and shaped into a special shape, a head dress for special occasions for the royalty and leadership.

Fez   **Dastaar**

Brother Elijah asked several questions regarding my knowledge on the subject. I said, "I had no idea why the Nizam wore it. I do recall he had another special cap that was uniquely different." Perhaps, the other cap was worn on special occasions. After all, they were of royal status. Nizam's oldest two sons married two Turkish princesses who were first cousins. The older son, Prince Azam Jah's bride was Princess Durru Shevar Sultan, the daughter of Sultan Abdulmejid. The younger son, Prince Mauzam Jah's bride was Princess Nilofer, daughter of the Sultan's brother. Both women were very beautiful, elegant and enterprising. It was a good feeling to know that I shared a birthday, with Princess Durre Shehvar's son, Prince Mukarram Jah that happened to fall on the day of the New Year – *"Nowruz",* the Persian New Year according to the Persian calendar. The Persian calendar, also known as the "Solar Hijri Calendar" was officially used in the State of Hyderabad, the Princely State of India. The Ruler was a Muslim and the population majority were 70% Hindu. Kashmir is the second Princely state in India ruled by a Hindu. The majority of the population is Muslim. It is interesting to know that Solar Hijri calendar means that its time reckoning is based on the earth's movements around the Sun. Unlike the Gregorian calendar, which follows a set of predetermined rules to stay in sync with the solar year, the Solar Hijri calendar is based on astronomical observations.

Invitations to the young prince's celebration included children of Nizam's advisors and staff. The children were elated to receive party favors and presents. The Party favors were small toys and candy treats, packed neatly in classic Christmas Stockings shaped mesh bags. Children also had fun dressing up in anticipation for the grand celebration.

The two Ottoman Princesses in the foreground. Princess Durru Shehvar in Center right and Princess Niloufer on her left.

On their left, two children are, my brother Emad Khaja wearing a Fez (Rumi Topi) and I, attending a birthday celebration of Princess Durreshahwar's son, Mukarram Jah, with children of Nizam's Advisory Staff by special invitation.

The conversation shifted and Brother Elijah talked about the shape and color of the Fez as we all joined the conversation. I then asked Sister Clara for a pad of paper and pencil and thanked her when she brought it to me. I said "Brother, if I may, I would like to show you the shape that would be great for you." Brother Elijah waited patiently for me. I sketched a hat/cap and embellished it with a prominent Crescent and Star and added scrolls and designs around it.

A Starry Crown - Making of a Fez

Original sketches of the Fez - Designs by Shakeela Z. Hassan

One of the originally proposed design-sketches for the Fez

Photo Credit and Source: Shakeela Z Hassan, Designer

One of the originally proposed design-sketches for the Fez

Photo Credit and Source: Shakeela Z Hassan, Designer

A STARRY CROWN

Brother Elijah was intrigued with the design and Sister Clara smiled in agreement. Sister Clara's smile and her happy demeanor were always a sign of her support and enthusiasm. Zia was also impressed with what his wife, me, was up to. All seemed content and ready for this project and it just got its start: *"In the Name of God, Amazingly Merciful, Infinitely Compassionate"*. We did not anticipate talking about a Fez project today, Making of the Fez was not envisioned, in plans or even in our thoughts. Here is how it all began: "A Fez was in the making!"

Brother asked, "Why the crescent and star and other designs?" I said, "Brother, the Crescent and Star, resembles the flags of Pakistan and Turkey, indicating the Islamic identity of the two countries. Turkey opted for color red and Pakistan chose green. The other designs are extra details. I like it because they are a part of Islamic arts and architecture. It brings character to the design which will also give you a distinct identity as the leader of an Islamic group."

Universally, Crescent Moon is the earliest moon of the Lunar Cycle and serves as a significant role for Islamic calendar settings. Lunar Cycle is a 14-day cycle and is the aberrant factor to predict the occurrence of the beginning of Ramadan and other important dates and events of celebration. Gregorian Calendar is based on Solar cycles and the dates on the two calendars do not concur on the same dates; there is a ten-day gap between the two, making it significant dates in Islamic practices as it appears repeatedly each year on the regular Gregorian calendar in use.

Brother Elijah, Sister Clara, Zia, and I were engrossed in our conversation as we anticipated the planning phase of the Fez. Our thoughts remained positive as we reflected on its completion. *"Better believe, it was meant to be!"*

Shakeela Z. Hassan, MD

Marshall Fields

It is interesting as to how the City of Chicago, and its signature store of the time with the iconic image of the CLOCK became part of our affinity for Chicago. This is the first place that came to mind and the only place Zia and I went shopping for the fabric we chose for Fez-making, the only fabric that came to mind, and agreed upon in unity by all and purchased at Marshall Fields and got made into a Fez. In fact, there was no discussion or consideration of any other options. Beautifully, as it turned out, Velvet seemed to be our collective choice, and remained to be the one forever after.

Marshall Field & Company

111 N. State Street, Chicago

Quietly, we left to go to the store. As we got in our car, Zia asked, "What is next?" I said, "Let us stop at Marshall Fields on State Street, at State and Washington." We parked in the car-park on Randolph Street and went into the store, taking the elevator to the fourth floor. This is where the fabrics are located, I indicated to Zia. Fabric sections were always my favorite, but not particularly Zia's. I was just glad he went with me. We looked through the finest velvet plush fabrics and selected the black silk velvet one. After measuring the approximate yardage, we purchased the fabric.

I embodied the calmest excitement and could hardly wait to start making the Fez. I could never call it a Fez, but I said to myself that is what it will be because Brother Elijah calls it a Fez, and it is to be worn only by him alone. Believe it or not, this was all done within half a day.

It is an inspiring thought to believe that "God helps those who help themselves." *"Insha'Allah, God Willing."* This phrase is not just a slogan, but speaks about faith and focus, making clear the role of the believer and their focus and fortitude.

As I have shared my chances, encounters and thoughts, it is important to mention that Zia and I never questioned our purpose or wondered about the meaning of… "Was it meant to be?"

Zia and I got home later with black silk velvet fabric and a paper sketch of a Fez in our hands to be made.

We both decided to make some phone calls. In doing so, we discovered that one of our contacts was travelling to Lahore Pakistan. We did not know them personally, but requested that they carry our closed package containing the fabric, my sketches for the embroidery, and the detailed description of the embroidery/embellishments. I was familiar with and very fond of a Hyderabadi classic, a special type of embellishment called *"Karchobi Work,"* a top favorite Zardozi style of work using Gold Thread, especially on Velvet fabric.

The Fez was finally taking shape. Zia took the measurements of Brother Elijah's head, right at the table. This process involved careful planning for such an important undertaking. A chance encounter and an 'Aha' moment bore witness to a legacy unfolding right before our eyes. This was a leader who engaged in social reform and loved to uplift and engage the human spirit, he called "The Black Man". He seemed always ready to share just one more time at every opportune moment: "Take charge, Be Responsible, Have Self-Respect, Be Self-Reliance, Know the Value of Self-Help, Do your share, Live Clean, Get Educated, Work Hard, Take care of Family, Eat Well, Know What you Eat, Be Prudent, Be Righteous", and so much more as if to say:

"Live a Life of Honesty and Responsibility!"

I am grateful to Sister Clara for providing a thick string to serve as a measuring tape and sample caps from Brother's stock for guidance. I was surprised how much Zia knew about the details of a cap/hat/Fez as we happily worked together. He shared his opinion about the appropriate height for the Fez, the strength of the lining and what would work best. Zia took the measurements of the Hon. Elijah Muhammad's head for the Fez, saving the measured string pieces. We brought it home and then Zia meticulously made sure he had his measuring-stick (ruler) to record the numbers "in inches" for sending to Pakistan.

Within a few weeks our plans were executed. We received three caps – one had a leather lining, as was customary in their hat-making industry. The leather was soft, but did not seem comfortable enough to wear on the head. "Let us not use the leather lining because in different weather conditions it is not the best on your head," said Zia. He said, "Let us use buckram, the stiff cotton, e.g., linen or horsehair cloth with a loose weave, often called muslin." He knew what Buckram was and how it was used in tailor-made suit collars and cuffs. We later learned that millinery buckram was different from the book binding buckram, a fabric impregnated with starch and was available in three different strengths; namely baby buckram, the softest, single ply buckram and double buckram (known as theatrical crown).

Finally, the Fez was created. Zia and I never forgot the day we took it to Brother Elijah and watched him put it on his head. With his characteristic smile, he snickered with sheer delight. We all were ecstatic with the outcome. The Fez was much needed, it was the right thing to do. Happily, it was well-received by the Leader and his community. The time frame that elapsed from the onset of the idea to the deliberation of the Fez, and Hon. Elijah Muhammad to have worn it with a very special pride and special joy, occurred well within the span of one year. It is surreal and serendipitous that this random chain of events deliberated in the making of the Fez. It seemed to be *"God's Will,"* indeed. Its place and strength over six decades and marching on to an unforeseeable future speaks for how it was meant to be, serving a need for the Leadership of the Hon. Elijah Muhammad.

The Honorable Elijah Muhammad

Photo Source: Alif Muhammad, Sr., grandson of the Hon. Elijah Muhammad and President of HEMCC Foundation

Photographed by Jabir Herbert Muhammad, son of Hon. Elijah Muhammad

A STARRY CROWN

Sister Ethel Eaa Sharrieff and Sister Lottie Rayya Muhammad, daughters of The Honorable Elijah Muhammad, were constantly in their parent's home. They surveyed the Fez by checking out the details and construction. Sister Ethel Eaa Sharrieff was an expert seamstress and played a major role in establishing the dress-making factory and its operation. She was Brother Elijah's older daughter. As the founder of the Nation of Islam's garment factory, she knew what buckram was and how she could make the Fez caps comfortable for her father.

Three embellished fabric pieces, each ready to be made into a Fez as need be, in Zia and Shakeela Hassan's possession waiting for the Call, "Sister Shakeela, It's time for a New Fez"

Photo Credit and Source: Shakeela Z. Hassan

Three embellished fabric pieces, each ready to be made into a Fez as need be, in Zia and Shakeela Hassan's possession waiting for the call, "Sister Shakeela, It's time for a New Fez."

I was diligent in making sure I always had at least one or two in stock. We were able to produce at least twelve or fifteen black caps, one white and two or three brown ones. Later, we were able to produce some blue ones too. I kept the blue and brown ones in stock.

After figuring out the Fez making process and Sister Ethel Eaa Sharrieff taking the lead in production, our responsibility was to concentrate on buying the velvet fabric at Marshall Fields, drawing the design, detailing the specifications and sending it to Lahore Pakistan. We also made sure we had one or two in stock at all times. From then on, Sister Ethel Eaa, under her meticulous attention and care, was instrumental in making the Fez.

There were no formal agreements established. We just flowed as a team and made tremendous progress. The execution of "Making of The Fez" progressed smoothly as if a detailed and deliberate plan of action was in place. Its worthy of note to mention that it all happened then and there, even in a very short period of time.

By sharing the pictures of the inside details of an original we have with us, it speaks for the details of deliberations and execution of the "Making of The Fez" Story.

One of the very first originals and its interior photographs are shared below. This is a historical fact preserved for the place it was designed and the name of the shop that continued to produce the subsequent models as required.

Photo Credit and Source: Shakeela Hassan

Shakeela Z. Hassan, MD

Photo Credit and Source: Shakeela Hassan

Photo Credit and Source: Shakeela Hassan

CHAPTER 4

The Journey Begins

My journey began in June 1956, after graduating from the Osmania University School of Medicine, Hyderabad, British India. That was the first time in my life, I travelled away from home. I travelled from Hyderabad India on a plane to London, then aboard the ship liner, SS Île de France (French- literally meaning, "Island of France") to New York, then aboard a Greyhound bus to Chicago and a Taxi ride to my destination, 2650 Ridge Avenue, Evanston, Illinois to the Northwestern University Hospital. My voyage ended one beautiful morning in June, as an announcement was made over the loudspeaker regarding the ship reaching its destination in a few hours. As our ship coasted towards the shore, the hours seemed long. The sun was shining bright and the lady of liberty's crown beamed in the sunlit glory — my heart pounded faster because I was not sure if I wanted this awesome wonder to end. Most of the passengers on the decks were excited, eager, and energized and looked forward to a new life and the journey of a lifetime that lay ahead. Once we reached New York, there were several transportation options available to us to reach our final destination. The crew discussed our options beforehand. With excitement, I said, "I would like to travel by Greyhound — chuckling to myself and remembering 'Leave the Driving Us — Take the Greyhound Bus." I would be in Chicago in twenty-four hours, as it was projected. I thought, "Wouldn't it be great to experience travelling via the highways and toll ways?" I was ready to experience the sights and the sounds and enjoy whatever else that lies ahead.

Post-Graduate Medical Training

The purpose of my visit to Chicago was for postgraduate medical training at Northwestern University's Evanston Hospital as an intern. After I graduated from Osmania University Medical School, I decided to apply for graduate training or medical residency opportunities in the USA. Chicago was my choice, as it seemed like a great city with several great medical schools and, more importantly, it was close to the states of Ohio and Indiana, where my two younger brothers were undergraduate students. The older one, Emad Khaja went to Tristate College and Earlham College, in Ohio, studying architecture, to and the younger one, Farees Khaja, went to Perdue University in Lafayette, Indiana to study Aeronautical Engineering.

As I began my internship in Evanston hospital, my recurring chance encounters made my commitment to work challenging. However, I was determined to work hard, learn and gain strength and confidence to be the best I could be and progress in my endeavors.

One day, the hospital administrator called me into his office. He asked, "Shakeela, what do you do to relax and have fun. Do you have any friends outside of the hospital?"

I was touched by his concern and care. I responded, "No I do not know anyone. The medical rotation was a very busy time and it certainly was strenuous yet rewarding experience for learning." He interrupted to repeat how they all were impressed by my hard work and interest. I thanked him and said, "I am pleased to have had this opportunity, and I love the experience. Brief time breaks help me catch some sleep. I also use that time to prepare for my daily academic and clinical assignments. In the busy time, I am referred to get involved in my first assignment of working in the Polio ward." There was a Polio epidemic at that time. I was sequestered – in other words, I was on duty, positioned in the Polio ward around the clock. My meals were served there and I slept in one of the cubicles in the ICU Ward, as time permitted. The hospital administrator was very much concerned about me, as a foreign medical graduate working tirelessly and now sequestered in a medical ward full of acutely ill patients during a Polio epidemic. (The real reason for my need to stay in isolation with my patients was because I had not received the Polio Vaccine - oral at the time. Now, I was in direct contact with Polio patients and at risk of contracting Polio myself.) But in about 2-3 weeks, the Polio epidemic was under control.

I was fascinated to learn and participate in the ventilator care and all other challenging situations encountered. Most noteworthy was the Director and Program Chairman of the Polio Ward, Dr. Martin Seifert, who had me accompany him to Cook County Hospital's Polio Ward as he made his rounds there too. First in the ward, he took me to the basement of Evanston Hospital. Pointing to a large barrel shaped ventilator he said "Here is the Iron Lung" – I had never seen this machine, not even a picture of it, let alone knowing how to make it work! He gave me a stack of papers and said, "Here is the Mimeographed copy of the iron lung manual – just read it and figure out how to work it. We are expecting patient admissions at any time **now.** There is a pregnant patient amongst the expected arrivals and she will need to undergo a Caesarian section soon." This made me concerned and nervous, especially when I realized that no one seemed to be an expert on the subject who could take the lead and teach me more. Anyhow, I said to myself, "Where there is a will, there is a way". Thankfully, my father who lived in England as a student and his love for the English language, literature, etiquette, poetry and quotations, did set the stage and direction for me.

To prepare myself for the assignment, I was blessed to have a small group of house staff to work with me as a team. I found myself actively engaged by working with others in our pursuit to learn and do our best to provide care and healing for the patients. The most memorable assignment was when I was allowed and given the opportunity to assist in a Cesarean section delivery of a woman who was on ventilator assistance in the Iron lung.

In retrospect, there was no need for me to fear or worry. My perspective changed as I realized, I was a silent, polite and respectful observer. I moved ahead with precision and worked hard to do my best and learn all I could. These were all great learning experiences that strengthened me. In hindsight could this encounter be predicting my future carrier to be a tenured faculty member of Anesthesiology and Critical care, at the University of Chicago for decades and retiring as an Emeritus faculty? Yet, the most important thing was learning the power of prayer and gratitude which has helped me tremendously in life and my medical career. I learned, it is all about the process and not a quick fix. At every juncture, there is a need for improvement. Spiritual awakening is a process it's not just incidental. The more awareness one receives, the greater his instincts will increase and along comes God's blessing and Mercy.

The administrator's call, conversation and an invitation to attend the Illinois Institute of Technology was a part of God's plan. He said, "There is a Professor at IIT who is inviting a group of foreign students from the Chicago area to join him and his wife for dinner. He lives on campus". Imagine the late 1950s, where a group of ten or twelve foreign students, including me — a resident physician in training, were sought after and invited to Chicago's south side! A foreign student? Me? How amusing! I wasn't familiar with this terminology. I went with another foreign female student to the apartment building on IIT campus.

Little did I know, this was the predestined place where Zia and I were to meet, get married, reside in this building and raise our family. A string of momentous surprises continued to unfold as time swiftly moved forward. Never to be forgotten are the treasured memories of our marriage in December 1959 which was held in the lobby of Carmen Hall, a campus residence hall where Zia and I lived in our earlier years of marriage. On December 18th, Zia Hassan and I got married – another historic milestone for us. Zia Hassan met Jamil Diab, an Arabic teacher in the Nation of Islam schools and asked him to perform our Nikaah, a Muslim ceremony and marriage contract. My maternal uncle, Karamat-ullah, a graduate student at the University of Chicago, served as an elder for me, substituting the presence of my parents. My two younger brothers, several friends, co-workers, Embassy of Pakistan officials from Washington DC, and a group of visiting delegates from Pakistan's WAPDA project were the happy guests. Additionally, my Attending physicians, Zia's professors, more friends and families happily joined the guest list.

Zia was one of the IIT students invited to the group dinner. He was a graduate student in the Department of Industrial Engineering. He worked for Webcor Corporation in St. Charles Illinois, and was also a teaching assistant. He seemed like a very busy person, but he made time for me. I felt as if I was not alone in this journey. The meaning of our momentous encounters speaks for itself. In this dinner he mentioned that Pakistan Independence event on August 14th, 1956 was taking place at the University of Chicago's International House. I did join him there. During that evening, he invited me to join him to visit a family in Chicago's south side, Brother Elijah and his wife Sister Clara Muhammad. He said he met them right after he came to Chicago and visited them with his older brother, Dr. Ijaz ul Hassan, who had met him in a clinic/hospital a year back. He referred to them as Brother and Sister and I just followed suit with the salutation. We continued to address them as such and as a symbol of our special respectful and fond relationship. He did say they were black Muslims and from the Nation of Islam.

CHAPTER 5

Extraordinary Encounters of my Ordinary Life

As part of my introduction to America, another story unfolded. One evening, I vividly remember receiving a telephone call from the Chief Resident. This occurred in the middle of July 1956. He said, "Please come down right away to the surgeon's lounge for an urgent meeting." I hurriedly gathered my things and made my way there. As I approached the lounge, I discovered that the door was closed. Was I in the right place? I said to myself. After a brief pause, I knocked, and someone opened the door. Hmm… It sure was dark in there. Suddenly the lights were turned on and a group of thirty or more resident physicians screamed in unison "Ta Qui Laaaaaaaaaa!".

I was highly amused. Was that supposed to be my name? I did not have to wonder for long why I was there. A liquor bottle was placed in the center of the table which was adorned with a green operating room sheet. I laughed and said, "Thank you, now you know my name, but you will know it better when I spell it for you. I am sure you will never forget – My name is S.H.A.K.E.E.L.A!" Who is next I asked! In my attempt to somehow respond to the "drinking" scenario, I said, "sorry I do not drink alcohol."

They said "we are only celebrating you!"

"Oh God", I said in my heart, I do know this custom. I have seen it in films. They all chanted–NO! NO! NO! Your glass is empty. I said, "I do not drink alcohol and I have decided not to start things that I cannot keep up with." I wondered and knew this was the beginning of a new journey of discovery and debate. So, the wise choice to make is to do what you think is right.

Nobody had a name even close to being so exotic! I was asked what my name was in English and what I would like to be called. Then I was asked, "How did you learn English so fast?" "Did you learn to speak English in England?" "Do you eat tomatoes?" "Do you have roses?" and more questions followed – I guess to simply get to know me!

We all walked over to the cafeteria where I was presented as "the celebrated guest, I assumed with an exotic name." "What would you like to eat? Hamburger, Hot Dog, Macaroni and Cheese?" I said, "I would like to have the last option." When asked why not the other choices, I said, "I do not eat ham, pork or bacon." Why? Because I am not supposed to, according to my religion.

"Are you a Mohammedan?" I said, "You are right to think that way. As Christians are followers of Christ, and you believe as Prophet Muhammad's followers, we must be Mohammedans. We are simply referred to as Muslims. Also, we are the followers of the religion Islam, and believe in all the Prophets – from Adam to Muhammad – and believe him to be the last Prophet and routinely say Peace be Upon him after taking their name for all the Prophets".

Then the discussion circled back to why I couldn't eat pork, ham or bacon. Hamburger? I said I do not eat ham. Hot Dogs? I said that sounds horrible. Too many questions, but I did not feel disgruntled or exasperated. I did feel disappointed and surprised at how little they knew about me.

On the other hand, I was glad I was asked these questions. I was happy to provide answers to the best of my ability and was pleased that we were learning together, "learning about each other." To my surprise, another fellow house staff member stopped them all. He came close to me and put his arm around my shoulder and said in a firm tone of voice, "Stop right there!" adding – "Do not harass her, do not ask her why she does not eat those meats, as I don't either. I understand why. I am Jewish and I follow the same guidelines. We are cousins." This started my journey to interfaith education, getting to know one another, celebrating our differences and treat each other with dignity. This took root in my life as I become committed to learning more. This was my introduction to Jewish Muslim dialogue and friendship.

We all laughed, and this only brought us closer, free of conscious reluctance, suspicion and being strange, which eased the discomfort and anything else that could have resulted. A clear vision of being friends in faith and bonded by a shared element – being HUMAN! Confirming the truth of a well-known cliché, "laughter is the best medicine". Wow, I thought! How wonderful to discover different healing methods? I feel so blessed to know that there are other remedies that heal besides the act of prescribing medicines – basic human encounters and interactions. Listen! Hear! Experience!

Shakeela and Zia Hassan's marriage, December 18th, 1959

Mr. Jamil Diab and his family with Zia and Shakeela Hassan

Dr. Jamil Diab officiated the Nikaah, Islamic wedding Ceremony, for the couple and was an Arabic Teacher at the Sister Clara Muhammad Schools in Chicago

CHAPTER 6

The Final Outcome

My father loved photography. During his stay in England before returning home to Hyderabad, British India and settle down, get married and have a family, he had a big win in his first visit to a horse race. That started his passion to focus on his interest in photography. I was his first subject hence can share to have had largest number of photos as an infant and as toddler and older.

Recently, I came across one in a collection that speaks volumes of what I recognized. I shared the photo with my friend, Halimah Muhammed Ali, the granddaughter of Brother Elijah Muhammad and Sister Clara Muhammad, daughter of Sister Lottie Rayya and her husband. Sister Lottie was the younger one among the two daughters of Brother Elijah and Sister Clara. Sister Lottie Rayya was the fifth sibling of eight children. Sister Halimah and I were engrossed in the conversation about her dear grandmother, Sister Clara Muhammad whom I lovingly referred to as my sister, and my friend. We both had the same thought concerning a specific photograph from my childhood. I said, "Halimah, Look at this picture. My mother dressed me up for some special occasion, didn't she? Is the cap on my head an indication that I will be Making One when I grow up?"

The design and embroidery on my cap seemed to be predicting to serve as a "Fez Designer" when she grows up. Is this how the Making of the Fez, took shape at an appropriate time and for a special person and again for a particular purpose? It is serendipitous that Fez Making for The Honorable Elijah Muhammad was in my cards, in my future, except that I had no idea, not a clue, not an intention till Zia joined me in this process and we were together with Hon. Elijah and sister Clara Muhammad in their home, at their Dinner table!

Wearing a cap was not a part of my regular wardrobe at home, in school or in any other setting. Neither do I recall its significance. I am sure though that it could have a ceremonial value of sorts. It surely had the embroidery; seemingly indicative of the wearing toddler becoming a Fez designer for The Honorable Elijah Muhammad.

Shakeela Hassan as a toddler photographed by her father, Hameduddin Khaja

Shakeela Hassan as a toddler photographed by her father, Hameduddin Khaja

Finally, the process was about to take shape and make progress.

The Fez, its symbolic design and an iconic mark of distinction for the leader, serving as an honor of identity and distinguished presence amongst leaders both locally and globally.

Occasionally, Brother Elijah indicated to us both with his characteristic smile. "It's time for a new Fez". As I recall, every so often Brother Elijah Muhammad referred to his Fez as the Starry Crown.

He knew and always smiled in anticipation of our response:

"Yes Brother, we have them".

Photo Credit and Source: Shakeela Z. Hassan

We kept no formal counts or records. Simply in good faith and with good intentions of its remarkably spontaneous random, Fez got made. We always had some in stock to supply the need to just have another new one, again in good faith, sense of family and friendship with good intentions and as an expression of our high regards, respect, admiration for Brother Elijah and Sister Clara. Their loving trust and honored relationship with us and their devotion and dedication to care and commitment for uplifting of the fellow beings, especially as Brother Elijah always mentioned, the Black man referring to the Black Community was a joy to behold.

Brother Elijah had much love for Zia. He had high regards and total comfort with Zia's simplicity, and his unassuming, selfless and respectful support for Brother Elijah's message in 'Doing Right and Being Righteous', which was the basis of mutual trust and comfort. These were the basics that brought us both a lifetime of love and ongoing relationship, with not just Brother Elijah and his dear wife, Sister Clara Muhammad, but their eight children, two daughters (Sister Ethel Eaa Sharieff, Sister Lottie Rayya Muhammad) , six sons (Brothers Emmanuel, Nathaniel, Herbert Jabir, Elijah II, Wallace Warith Dean and Akbar Muhammad), as well as across the generations – grandchildren and their children and some of the extended family members (Hafeezah Gail Bahar); older grandsons (Br. Jabir's sons: Elijah, Jesus, Sultan and Alif; Sister Lotties's sons: Wali and Ameer).

With the passage of time it is with special kinship and fondness I mention my friends, the granddaughters Halimah Mohammed-Ali, Zainab Sharieff, Aleatha Sharieff and Safiyya Mohammad Rahma, and Amal A. Muhammad. I feel happy to add that Sister Ethel Eaa Muhammad's four daughters, and Sister Rayya Lottie's two daughters, accompanying their mothers, were a frequent presence at their Grandparents' home.

A STARRY CROWN

Our friendship with Br. Jabir Herbert, his wife, Sister Amenah Antonia Muhammad, extends to relationships with their sons Sonny Elijah Muhammad III, Alif Muhammad Sr., Isa Muhammad Ali, *Late* Br. Sultan Muhammad, *Late* Br. Sultan's son, Sultan Rahman Muhammad and grandson Sultan Sadeeq Muhammad; Sister Lottie Rayya Muhammad's sons *Late* Wali Muhammad and Ameer Muhammad.

CHAPTER 7

What Does Lady Liberty Have to Say?

The emerging image of the Statue of Liberty in the New York Harbor, a 151 feet tall structure, is a sign of welcome, hope and invitation for enlightenment and education. I was touched and inspired as I learned about President Roosevelt's speech, which filled me with emotions, pride, honor and inspiration. During the rededication of the Statue of Liberty and to mark the monument's 50th anniversary, FDR said, *"For over three centuries a steady stream of men, women and children followed the beacon of Liberty which this light symbolizes. They brought to us strength and moral fiber developed in a civilization, centuries old but fired anew by the dream of a better life in America."*

While in New York, my primary reason for the visit, as a recent graduate of medical school, was to pursue postgraduate education and training. A question of whether I thought about a future beyond this, or if I could predict becoming an American Citizen, was not clear in my consciousness. Knowing myself, my professional progress coupled with the unexpected random twists and turns, I can honestly say I am convinced it was all predestined and was just a matter of time before it all came to fruition. What was lying dormant inside of me propelled me forward, enabling me to witness God's guidance as a blessing in disguise. My ordinary life was beginning to unfold as it was destined to.

I am so grateful for the blessing of comfort given by a man of humility, my husband Zia. I am blessed that over six decades Zia and I continued to be a team of two, working, and serving together doing the best we could. In the REAL Man's world of yester years in Academics and other aspects of life, Zia's support was key for me to blessed with extraordinarily momentous encounters and opportunities in my ordinary life. Blessed are the simple humans, focused in servitude, Thanks Be to God, *Alhamdulillah!*

I tried to not dwell on the fact that I was a foreign student, a foreign medical graduate, or an immigrant. Instead, my focus centered on being a woman, a Muslim woman. Am I an Indian or Pakistani? I identified with Hyderabad, British India because I was not yet a Pakistani citizen. Later, a terminology that became popular to define such dilemmas was "Indo Pakistani". If I were to migrate to Pakistan, I would be labeled as a Mohajar – meaning an immigrant. Later, I achieved Pakistani citizenship through naturalization. In 1979, I became a United States Citizen, a proud one at that. I was also asked if I am a Mohammedan, and my reply was "yes". "Christians are the followers of Christ, 'Oh Well'. "A follower of Mohamed, assumed therefore, is Mohamedan" To understand where that thought was coming from was more important than to just decide, "They are --------- This or that."

We are all Human, after all – has been brewing in my system to benefit from experiential learning opportunities—how fortunate to not just face questions but to have opportunities to address from my comfort of discovery, and learnings of my very own faith and values. Blessing it has been on experiential learning pathways learn and deliberate attempts at Uniting and building peace, justice, and a compassionate coexistence for our diverse human family.

Muslims complete the Three Abrahamic Faiths. The Prophets we have in common are all mentioned in the Qur'an from Abraham to Moses and Jesus. Muhammad is the last Prophet who received the Revelation of the Qur'an while meditating in the Cave of Hira in Arabia. Decades later, the hyphenated existence continues its enrichment. With pride and joy these hyphenations are sources of my fulfilment in allowing me to be me. They need to know others as you get to know yourself has become the theme of my life and inspiration. Experiential learning began for me over sixty years ago with my partner in life, love and learnings, my husband, Zia Hassan. He was my pillar of strength, a source of my sustenance, my pride and joy. Our story has been a journey in faith, learning and trying to do our best. While never achieving perfection, it has been a rewarding journey of blessings indeed.

Zia enjoyed sharing his favorite line, "*Life is a journey of on-going quality improvement.*" I share again as I believe, it so much in sync with our faith and reliance on: "The Oneness of God & One Humanity." Serve God as you serve fellow humans.

I thought about being American and wondered what that meant. Is America a land of opportunity – a safe place to be which provides a sense of security regardless of your color or creed, faith or familiarities, gender or genealogy?

I find President Roosevelt's speech profound. Even though recent practices emphasize diversity in our nation, was it diverse yet distinguished or distinct being Christian?

Why discuss human values and humanity, if other faiths are left feeling adamant because of their differences? How can I call myself a Muslim if I have no clue as to how to be one? It became clear to comprehend and honestly pursue the discipline, devotion and deliberations in my life of being a Muslim: Paying attention to basic requirements became a way to define my journey of faith.

"One God, One Humanity" Qur'an addresses human beings as *"Ya aiyuhal Nas"* (O Humankind) directly 306 times and indirectly more than two thousand times in its over 6,000 verses. In contrast the Qur'an specifically addresses Muslim men and women (Ya aiyuhal Muslimun/Muslimat/Muslimatun/etc.) by name only 49 times.

"Yes, I can" became energized by the comfort knowing:

"God does not burden anyone more than one can bear" ~Holy Qur'an Surah Baqarah, 2:286

President Franklin D. Roosevelt's speech on October 1936 played a role in honor of the Statue's 50th Anniversary, and helped solidify the transformation of the Statue into an icon of immigration. In the speech, he presented immigration as a central part of the nation's past and emphasized the newcomers' capacity for Americanization. I was inadvertently on a path of celebration of my faith when destiny intervened to shape my present and future. My self-envisioned blessings were in alignment with my zodiac sign, Libra.

I am honored to be an American and thankful to President Franklin D. Roosevelt for his unwavering devotion to mitigate immigration laws.

For over three centuries a steady stream of men, women and children followed the beacon of Liberty which this light symbolizes. They brought to us strength and moral fiber developed in a civilization, centuries old but fired anew by the dream of a better life in America.

CHAPTER 8

Knowing Elijah and Clara Muhammad

Personal Reflections by

Shakeela Z. Hassan

Having never heard of The Nation of Islam, Black Muslims or even Africans in general, it was an extraordinary encounter and experience in the life of two young immigrant Muslims, Zia Hassan and Shakeela Hassan, to meet the Honorable Elijah and his wife Sister Clara Muhammad. From a chance first meeting to a lifetime spanning over decades and across generations, it was and continued being a precious gift, in its own span and significance. *"After all this time ~ Always" – J.K Rowling*

Zia came to Chicago from Lahore, Pakistan and I came from Hyderabad, British India. Here I have chosen to reflect on this journey, its lessons, and team-togetherness of a lifetime of our partnership and teamwork. I find how it fits in my need for reflection and how it became part of shaping our faiths, its strength, beauty, majesty and meaning for the two of us to be comfortable with a broader diverse human family, shouting out joyously, *"We are only humans, after all."* For my innate and perpetual need to belong, to be a part of and to work together with others, it served to restore respect, cultivate regard and make sense for relevance of compassion at a core of our co-existence, and I feel at my best being a part of a diverse human family. To me that meant not just local human family but a national family - an America of strength and potential. I could feel the need, the want and the struggle and strife these new friends, elders in our life were trying to fast forward to new heights as they were overcoming hatred, despise, deprivation and pure abuse and neglect.

I do not claim to have played a role in the formation of the Nation of Islam in Chicago or its membership or community. If it supported a momentum, a potential for the group, it was a pure chance – God's Will. It is with deep respect and honesty I can claim to have learned lessons, enjoyed all I witnessed and experienced "a work in progress, under God's Mercy, Guidance and Perpetual Blessing, for common Good". The grace and beauty have been to have witnessed firsthand, with the opportunity to ask questions, learn and be there whenever there was a need to serve sincerely, honestly and effectively, with no expected returns. This Fez Story is a unique example. Out of nowhere to somewhere, making room for The Leadership to evolve with distinction and elegance, the relationship has spanned over six decades, 1960 to today and will continue beyond, *God Willing.*

Earlier in the book I have shared notions of the encounters that brought Zia and me together, and us to Elijah and Clara Muhammad, even before my husband and I really knew each other to any degree. I had no questions or concerns to accompany a 'stranger' to go and visit them; he had comfort and fond regards for them and confidently explained to me, "I have met them and they are nice people and are keen to meet you." He added with comfort and conviction, "I know you would like them."

I have often wondered why it never came to my mind, what was he thinking, why I was being asked to meet a Black Muslim family, who were the Nation of Islam members and so much more. In my lifetime I had known or met only one other Muslim of African descent: Mrs. Maqbool when I was growing up. She was the wife of

Dr. Maqbool, a Hyderabadi gentleman, and his wife was a nice and well-liked African lady. Her race or religion did not prompt comment in the trivia of the times.

As we made it to 4847 South Woodlawn Avenue in Chicago's Hyde Park Kenwood neighborhood to the Elijah and Clara Muhammad residence, in about the end of August 1956, I had no idea if this might be the only visit for me.

In fact, visits became many, and ever more frequent with time. It was God's will all the way as time and its attestation has sailed by to convince each one of us that all that happens, happens with the will of God.

On December 18, 1959 Zia and I got married and went to see them. Whenever Brother Elijah and Sister Clara Muhammad felt there was a need to connect, converse or simply have dinner together, we visited. It was always a pleasure to visit when we could.

In this book I have shared how the Fez was an amazing story of randomized events and outcomes in history in accordance with God's Will and Human simplicity, to "Go with the flow" and "do the right thing from your heart, in faith and with honesty and honor."

My reflection is shared for the truth that encouraged and inspired to be blessed to know the righteousness, and the basics that we observed and were comfortable with knowing what our faith is, what our defined religion was evolving to be the goodness of our consciousness about being a Muslim and what made us essentially good.

Earlier in our visits I became aware of certain details of how Nation of Islam became a community of faith. I do not intend to elaborate details of history and development of faith and values and its defined perception in general across the land. Neither did I have a judgement of who is better than whom. In fact, as I learned from my parents how being good was not just the "goodness" of one particular group. Others were different but that did not mean they were all bad or inferior to us good folks.

There were opinions expressed on personal and media fronts as to the financial, educational and civic fronts in terms of Afro-African community. Most noteworthy was how Brother Elijah Muhammad seemed focused on his own commitment to raise the level of education, faith family values and sense of responsibility on all fronts. He would often use the word Devil in reference to the white man. I must say I was always welcomed by him personally to ask questions and he was comfortable to share his thoughts and meaning of whatever that came to my mind to ask. At times I felt like he wondered why I was not raising my hand and had no question to engage in conversation. I will share a few things that I clearly recall that I brought up and felt good knowing what he had in mind and how he processed his focus, thoughts, actions and commitments.

In the interest of keeping my reflection simple and what brought me to understand Elijah and Clara Muhammad, and the workings of the Nation of Islam on the social justice front, teaching of faith, and values and building of civic, social and family responsibilities, I will just share noteworthy encounters that brought regards and respect for this wonderful family.

Shakeela Z. Hassan, MD

Master Fard Muhammad

Suffice it to say I got the idea that Master Fard Muhammad was introduced to Brother Elijah Muhammad by his wife Sister Clara. Obviously, she felt that there was some good to be shared and knowing her own husband, and perhaps his focus on "Betterment of the Black Man."

I must clarify that being a young medical graduate did not mean I was a seasoned scholar of Islam, ethics or even doing good. But the energy of expression and shielding of my questions with calm, courteous attention and sharing "the truth" by brother Elijah Muhammad, made sense. What I recall is that "God visited in the person of Master Fard Muhammad". I was not comfortable with the thought and I just raised my hand to ask a question and Brother Elijah seemed always to be very kind to encourage me to speak, "my mind". I said, "Brother, God is not a person." It seemed like I was trying to share its meaning in my young and early understanding and trying to convey my thoughts in English. Brother said, as I remember, "God is One, God is everywhere, something like God is in everyone" or something like that. I am not sure how exactly I felt or could have or did say. I did learn that God's presence is everywhere but he does not appear in person like a human being. It is not just my imagination, but later in time

Master Fard and came to know that he had left.

The Name Elijah Muhammad

Master Fard Muhammad gave Elijah Poole a Muslim name, Elijah Muhammad, and then advised that righteous people should have righteous names. Unsettling to me was the thought Fard Muhammad advised Bro. Elijah Muhammad that he was to be Allah's Messenger and Prophet. I was disturbed in my heart and mind, "Oh God I pray this is not meant to imply that Elijah Muhammad is taking the place of Prophet Muhammad, peace be upon him." I kept asking, "Prophet Muhammad is the last prophet and politely referring to the thought that Brother Elijah was a prophet and in heart I was hoping and praying, the last Prophet, a Prophet for our faith, Islam was not being replaced." I believed that Brother Elijah was coming to his own understanding, focus and teachings for the community as he was clarifying his own expression, his message to the Nation of Islam community. One could see the naturally evolving teachings, learnings and practices, fine-tuning perpetually. Here it is significant to say- I believe Learning is a process of reflection of one's ongoing and evolving character, conduct and commitment. I fondly recall it is another favorite quote from Zia Hassan's life, "Character, Conduct and Commitment". I also remember Brother Elijah Muhammad describing how prophets have come at different times. We had some discussion, conversation, back and forth as to how does one define messenger vs the Prophet. Slowly there was no frequent mention of being a messenger or a prophet and so on, and I honestly felt he was working on himself to present to his people what is right and he felt that he had to use the ways and means through which they will understand. That was the only practical and prudently honest way to do so. A quote comes to mind:

"If a Child Can't Learn the Way We Teach, Maybe We Should Teach the Way They Learn."
~Ignacio Estrada

Shakeela Z. Hassan, MD

White Man

I asked, "Brother why do we [my polite reluctance to not put to point fingers at him and his community] have to call them - those who you believe did wrong and continue to be disrespectful and hurtful - Devil." Brother continued, "Sister do you know they have practiced slavery, called us mindless, monkeys and not capable of doing anything, not deserving education and opportunity." I could feel the pain, the injustice and reality of how the wrong has progressed and 'prospered' and gained grounds to continue. His definite feeling was that first of all, his folks will not understand if they could not articulate, who need their focus to deliberately ignore and take charge of their very own self-respect, self-interest in education, initiatives, hard work and making progress on fronts of Self and simply taking charge of their faith, conduct and destiny.

Early on in Chicago, I experienced the Field Museum of Natural History, and for the first time. I was intrigued and inspired by human growth and development and also seeing how the human body evolved its size and shape, and how people twist evolution to abuse and insult others: crude, cruel and totally out of place. And to top it off hurtful and more so with unfair practices of not providing opportunities adequately and respectfully for one and all with discrimination and outright neglect. It is very thought-provoking for me to wonder how progressive and advanced the concept of education was in this household. In 1930's Sister Clara established a school in her own home. They together with their family and community widened the scope and opportunities across the United States with growing numbers and growing structures: preschools to the University level. I do not think the acknowledgements and publicity were contextual. Always overshadowed with negatives and presentation in light of prejudices and not with deserved dignity, quality or adequacy.

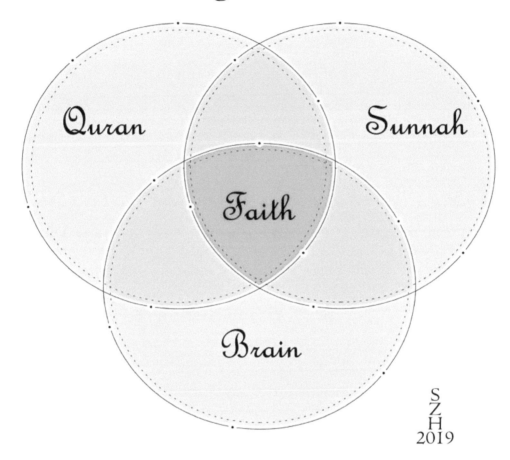

My Personal Concept of Being a Muslim

"Which of the favors of your Lord can you deny?" ~Holy Qur'an Surah Ar-Rahman 55:18

"Verily, with every hardship comes ease," ~Holy Qur'an Surah Ash-Sharh 94:6

In my youthful encounter with the seriousness of what, and why of religion, Islam was a wide-open arena for me to keep on learning and making sense. In fact, these thoughts served to be the basis for my understanding of the meaning of faith for me, in my heart. Reflection was a way and means to make sense in what I believe or should believe and live by, especially as a Muslim, Always remembering that Islam is not just a religion, it is a way of life, being cognizant that the Three Things that Mattered were Number 1: **Teachings of the Qur'an,** Number 2: **Teachings of the Sunnah** (Prophet's Life and Tradition, Number 3: **My Brain:** God's endowed Gift to me as a Human. The Basis of these is that each individual is responsible for his/her own deeds and to be a believer and keep on doing good, one has to take strides and strives of getting educated, informed with clarity of information and directive for one's own conduct and responsibilities.

Hypocrites

I heard the word hypocrite in conversations around the dinner table meetings and settings. It was not a familiar word in my vocabulary and I did not feel a need to use it, not knowing its meaning or the contexts in which it would come in handy.

I decided to ask the question, "Excuse me Brother, you often describe and talk about the hypocrites, in context perhaps with the White man that you refer to as Devil."

He said, "You know what is a Hypocrite? There are three signs: when he speaks lies, when he makes a promise he breaks it, and when he is trusted he betrays his trust." Then he will elaborate how the Black Man and his community have been treated, betrayed, and abused. They are frozen in their tracks and I want them to "rise and shine" take charge and be responsible for themselves. He will add:

"When someone does not treat you right, he will not teach you right"

It is not a surprise, yet a surprise that the spontaneously uttered response from Brother Elijah Muhammad as to "What is meant by calling someone a Hypocrite." The words echo in what exists in a classic citation in Prophetic tradition, Sunnah, *Sahih Bukhari.* It made sense to me as it was echoing how crucial it was to know that being HUMAN is key to be a Muslim. A comforting thought indeed and personally feel proud to be Muslim, and continue to struggle and strife, on a journey of faith and as my husband's quote brings me comfort and inspiration to happily repeat just one more time:

"Life is a Journey of Perpetual Quality Improvement" - after all!

Ramadan in December

Sometime in the 1960s, in the month of December, I came home from my work at the hospital after laying off from night duty, and my husband mentioned, "We are going to visit Brother Elijah and Sister Clara, will you be ok?" asking if I had gotten any sleep at work. I said, "Yes it will be fine, can we just go as I get ready." Well, we did get there mid-morning on that Sunday, and I felt for the first time hungry, outside my home as I was visiting there, not at a meal time. Brother Elijah was sitting at the dinner table and received Zia with a smiling *"Assalamualaikum".* I got to greet him and then I just went to the kitchen, assuming Sister Clara was there. She was there and came forward giving me a hug and saying *Assalamualaikum* with a welcoming smile. As soon as I felt at ease I said, "Sister, I am hungry, may I please have some cereal." I must say I had never ever done that not before nor after. I am sure this was a purposeful direction of some sorts for me to have this eye-opening encounter! Sister responded in soft-spoken tone, "Sister, it is Ramadan." I was struck with mixed emotions, questions and plain old complexity of the situation.

I am grateful for not having felt judgmental or angry. Surprisingly, I was not feeling too uncomfortable with the idea. I was becoming aware of my own religiosity or its goodness and learning the lessons of my life which had begun as a young child at home watching certain practice ideals and choices. Then meeting and marrying a man who was a simple a human being. This particularly energized my spirit to be more human, especially in the light of being a Muslim watching Elijah Muhammad and Sister Clara and their commitment to the basics of faith, family and all the concerns and commitments I did not feel the need to look into exactly how they are different or I/we are different just being Muslims.

The turmoil brought racing cascade of queries and scenarios in my mind. I started nervously possibly muttering, "I am so sorry, Ramadan was not long ago. This is December, umm, is it Ramadan now. Please no worries about my request for food." We both started heading toward the dining room to join Brother Elijah and Zia. I went directly to my seat. Brother Elijah had heard something going on in the kitchen; he was a very astute and attentive listener. He said. "Is everything alright Sister?" Next to me was sister Clara with a bowl of cereal, milk and honey – placing them on a placemat in front of me on the table.

I repeated to brother, "Everything is fine Brother. I did not realize it was Ramadan, and I asked Sister Clara for some cereal as I felt hungry this morning having worked long hours on duty last night." He got comfortable with his characteristic posture and smiled with a finger across his upper lip. "Yes Sister, we observe Ramadan in December." He waited for me to say something. After a pause I said, "The Lunar calendar is changing every year by about ten days and does not coincide with the regular (Gregorian) calendar. As Muslims, we find it hard to plan the start of Ramadan or Eid celebrations for family and community with the assurance of taking off from work or plan the events." He kept his smile and responded. "My people need to understand. They spend time, money that they don't have with effort all December long on overactivity on food, drugs, drinks and doing all the bad that comes along. They spend a lot of money to celebrate Christmas, buying "gifts" they cannot afford. Most of them don't even know what they are celebrating and why and its significance. They just go wild with all the evil that they can get involved in.

So, I encourage them to observe and celebrate Ramadan in December. I could not resist chiming in, "the weather is good, days are short, and fasting with no food or water is more 'doable'". I soon added, "What a great idea. In Islam there is so much flexibility, if you cannot pray, you can make up the prayers, if you cannot fast, you can make up or in special circumstances like supporting the needy in Ramadan to fast. If you cannot pray standing, pray sitting, lying down or even just by the moving of the eyelids even in paralyzed states." Oh my God, I was just pouring my heart and getting struck with how this amazingly intelligent man was working out the issues of faith and practices with simple and sound practice, plus alternative choices – still under the religiously recommended practice options. In his case he was inspiring, encouraging and training his community to think, learn and use their knowledge, ability, capacity and commitment to embrace it all as they build self-esteem, self-respect, self-initiatives and total sense of comfort and responsibility. I quickly remembered that when I was young and was keen to join the family to fast, I noticed we as children woke up for *Suhoor* the early breakfast and were encouraged to do our best even if we happily ate another meal or some food or drink during the day, limiting the consumed amounts, keeping it simple and "believing/pretending as if we made two fasts in one day"– feeling happy and not feeling how wrong we were that we had to "break" our fast in the middle because we were not able to fast or were doing wrong. The ownership pride of having fulfilled a need to fast in Ramadan does energize the actual practice to be ready for doing so at the right time and in the right way.

A quick recall down past my childhood, which brought me comfort to have a compassionate and realistic insight to what Brother's thought was to customize faith convictions and practices to a community that needed a special sense and means to be on a righteous path and tradition.

The echoes of "Be good, no wrong doings, be nice to your family, friends and neighbors" seemed to be gently ringing, down the memory lanes. A feeling of having made progress, having learned, having felt the energy of lessons learned and traversed on the path and passage of life. This served in retrospect and reflection of how true a perspective it is to reflect on a personal quote of my husband, Zia Hassan, I repeat, *"Life is a journey of Perpetual Quality Improvement."* I do like to add my own thoughts: We are humans and must not fear having weakness and continued making of mistakes. We are humans after all, have a lot to learn and continued or perpetual opportunities to mend and make quality of life. A blessing it is to repent, rely on God and be in prayer and gratitude. *God is Infinitely Merciful and Amazingly Compassionate.*

A STARRY CROWN

Hon Elijah Muhammad's Fez Collection

Top Favorites

Photo Credit: Alif Muhammad, Sr., grandson of the Hon. Elijah Muhammad and President of HEMCC Foundation

Shakeela Z. Hassan, MD

Photo Credit: Alif Muhammad, Sr., grandson of the Hon. Elijah Muhammad and President of HEMCC
Foundation

Photo Credit: Alif Muhammad, Sr., grandson of the Hon. Elijah Muhammad and President of HEMCC Foundation

Shakeela Z. Hassan, MD

Photo Credit: Alif Muhammad, Sr., grandson of the Hon. Elijah Muhammad and President of HEMCC
Foundation

Hon. Elijah Muhammad Wearing His Fez on Bool Covers He Authored

Book presented to Zia Hassan in 1960s – Signature is that of Hon. Elijah Muhammad

Photo Credit and Source: Shakeela Z. Hassan

Shakeela Z. Hassan, MD

Selected Book Covers of Hon. Elijah Muhammad, Wearing The Fez

Message to The Blackman In American by the Hon. Elijah Muhammad, Published in 1965

Photo Credit: Alif Muhammad, Sr., grandson of the Hon. Elijah Muhammad and President of HEMCC Foundation

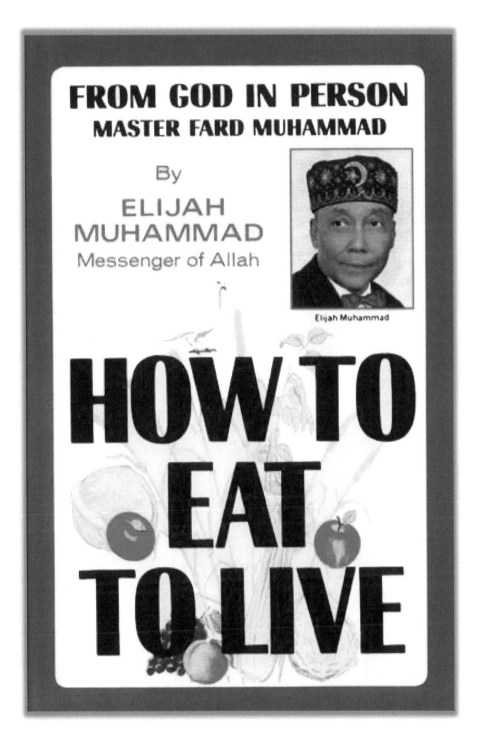

How to Eat to Live, by the Hon. Elijah Muhammad, Published in 1967

Photo Credit: Alif Muhammad, Sr., grandson of the Hon. Elijah Muhammad and President of HEMCC Foundation

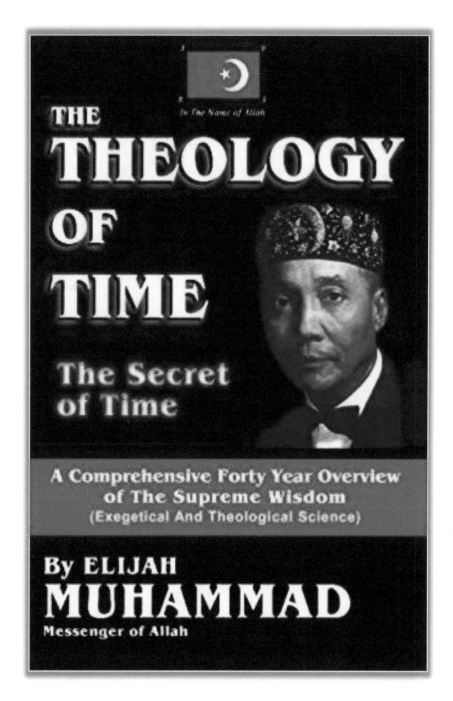

The Theology of Time, by the Hon. Elijah Muhammad, Published 1972

Photo Credit: Alif Muhammad, Sr., grandson of the Hon. Elijah Muhammad and President of HEMCC Foundation

A STARRY CROWN

Fez in the Exhibits

A starry-eyed young girl mesmerized looking at the Fez in a glass case display

(part of an exhibition in Detroit at the occasion of NOI Saviour's Day February 23-25, 2007 at

Charles H. Wright Museum.

Photographer: Monica Morgan

Photo Credit: Alif Muhammad, Sr., grandson of the Hon. Elijah Muhammad and President of HEMCC Foundation

Shakeela Z. Hassan, MD

Photographer: Amal A. Muhammad, 2007

(Grand-Daughter of Hon. Elijah Muhammad and daughter of *Late* Akbar Muhammad)

Photo Credit: Alif Muhammad, Sr., grandson of the Hon. Elijah Muhammad and President of HEMCC Foundation

"After Malcolm Project": Exhibition at Zuckerman Museum of Fine Art, 2014.

Photo Credit and Source: Dr. Abbas Barzegar and Thomas LaPorte

Shakeela Z. Hassan, MD

"After Malcolm Project": Exhibition at Zuckerman Museum of Fine Art, 2014.

Photo Credit and Source: Dr. Abbas Barzegar and Thomas LaPorte

Hon. Elijah Muhammad With Famous Black Leaders of His Time

The Hon. Elijah Muhammad with Dr. Martin Luther King in 1960's

Photo Credit: Alif Muhammad, Sr., grandson of the Hon. Elijah Muhammad and President of HEMCC Foundation

The Hon. Elijah Muhammad With Malcolm X in the 1960's

Photo Credit: Alif Muhammad, Sr., grandson of the Hon. Elijah Muhammad and President of HEMCC Foundation

The Hon. Elijah Muhammad with the Champ, Muhammad Ali 1960s

Photo Credit: Alif Muhammad, Sr., grandson of the Hon. Elijah Muhammad and President of HEMCC Foundation

Shakeela Z. Hassan, MD

A Final Tribute to the Making of the Fez

Its Iconic Presence for 60 Years

Being a Mark of Distinction and Evolution

Photo Credit: Guclu Koseli. Chicago Visual

A top favorite Fez, worn over time by Hon. Elijah Muhammad rests on a hand carved

Walnut Wood table from Lahore, Pakistan, in Zia and Shakeela Hassan's home

Photo Credit: Shakeela Z. Hassan

Acknowledgements

In no certain way can the list be complete to mention the role my family, friends and others have played in shaping the story of a lifetime for Zia and me. Simply in its historic perspective and significance, it has in every way served to be extra ordinarily gratifying in the lives of Zia and me and our partnered life ordinaire!

Thanks Be to God, Alhamdulillah!

We are humbly blessed and it is with gratitude I mention my family for their patience, support and love as our daughters, Rubeena Waqar Mian, Ayesha Z. Hassan and Isra Z. Hassan, witnessed our involvement our respect and relationship with Brother Elijah Muhammad, Sister Clara Muhammad and continuing with their eight children, grandchildren and great grandchildren even to this day.

I am also grateful to Elijah and Clara Muhammad family members for their love, respect, support and encouragement that this historic narrative be shared not just because it happened but how inadvertent, smooth and serene a journey it has been for us all. How natural, seamlessly and serenely human!

The history is better served in terms of respect and significance of journey and realization that, "whatever is meant to happen – does happen, as a testament to God's Will. Realization that the team effort of the players in the chance encountered moments are most humbling incidents in the lives of all in the journey.

Thanks Be to God, Amazingly Merciful and Infinitely Compassionate.

A STARRY CROWN

I most certainly acknowledge how grateful Zia and I are "to have been there, and continue. Not just witnessed, but became part of the shared encounters, actions and the details of the process, and the journey."

I begin with thanks to Alif Muhammad, Sr., son of the *Late* Brother Jabir Herbert Muhammad and his *Late* wife, Sister Amenah Antonia Muhammad, and grandson of Hon. Elijah and Sister Clara Muhammad, for decades long friendship with my husband, Zia Hassan and me. In addition, I gratefully acknowledge and appreciate provision of resource materials and photographs on behalf of his family and as president of HEMCC (Honorable Elijah Muhammad Commemorative Center Foundation). My thanks for Sister Najmah Qatadah Rasool for her encouragement and support. It is with wonder and a special sense of pride I mention Sultan Sadeeq Muhammad, a great-great grandson of the Hon. Elijah Muhammad, son of Sultan Rahman Muhammad. Who would've thought that he would be participating in this journey. My dear friend Professor Winni Fallers Sullivan, and her invaluable encouragement, patience, support and friendship deserves a special mention. Her article "Shakeela Hassan", perhaps was the energy that moved me forward to take this step!

Last but not the least – little girl Halimah, a starry eyed, beautiful, six-year old, who shared a mutually captured moment on our first ever meeting at the "HOUSE" in August 1956 – a family historian since then, is on top of my long list of acknowledgements and gratitude for this journey of my lifetime! The encountered moments, as fresh as any human experience gets!

Thanks Be to God, Alhamdulillah!

Shakeela Z. Hassan, MD

About the Author

Shakeela Zia Hassan is a philanthropist, interfaith community organizer, and retired medical professional living in Chicago, Illinois. Hassan came to America from Hyderabad, British India, as a young medical graduate in 1956 for postgraduate education, starting an internship at Northwestern University Hospital, and eventually gaining a teaching appointment at the University of Chicago Hospitals. After four decades of patient care and clinical leadership, she retired as Associate Professor Emeritus of Anesthesiology and Critical Care.

As a young woman new to Chicago's South Side, her husband-to-be Zia Hassan introduced her to Elijah Muhammad and Sister Clara Muhammad and their eight children. As Shakeela relates, Clara Muhammad was "nothing short of a mother to me". Their relationship was born in an important moment where divisions between "immigrant and indigenous" Muslims in the United States were less important than their shared faith.

In addition to their friendship, Shakeela shared elements of South Asian Islamic heritage with Elijah Muhammad, from recipes and prayers to textiles. The story of the caps she created for him – his "Starry Crown," worn in some of the best-known images and moments of his leadership – provides a rare glimpse not only into his personality, but into a bygone era of Muslim and American solidarity that has much to teach us. (As told by Shakeela through anecdotes and archival materials, Sister Clara's own vision illuminates this important history with grace and humility).

Bibliography

Bernard A. Zuckerman Museum of Art, Kennesaw, Georgia: "After Malcolm Project Exhibit". 2014. Courtesy Dr. Abbas Barzegar & Thomas LaPorte. www.aftermalcolm.com.

Charles H. Wright Museum of African American History., Detroit, Michigan. NOI Historical Exhibition on Saviour's Day, 2014. Courtesy Alif Muhammad Sr., grandson of the Hon. Elijah Muhammad and President of HEMCC Foundation.

Muslim Journal. "A Special Daughter in the Clara Muhammad/Elijah Muhammad Family "Shakeela Hassan"". Vol. 43, 3 Nov. 2007.

Roosevelt, Franklin D., "Address on the Occasion of the Fiftieth Anniversary of the Statue of Liberty." *The American Presidency Project*, 28 Oct. 1936. Online by Gerhard Peters and John T Wooley. https://www.presidency.ucsb.edu/documents/address-the-occasion-the-fiftieth-anniversary-the-statue-liberty. Accessed 6 Dec. 2019 (cited on p. 65).

Sapelo Square. "Dr. Shakeela Hassan and the Making of an American Muslim Icon" 4 Nov. 2018. https://sapelosquare.com/2018/11/14/dr-shakeela-hasan-and-themaking-of-an-american-icon/.

Sullivan, Winnifred Fallers. *Frequencies* "Shakeela Hassan". 20 Sept. 2011. frequencies.ssrc.org.